TEXAS ALPHABET

WRITTEN AND ILLUSTRATED BY
LAURIE PARKER

"True work is about enchantments." — Meister Eckhart

Acknowledgments
Thanks to Annette Goode and Sheila Williams for always being supportive,
and special thanks to Cyndi Clark for doing a terrific job on layout!!

Photographs of Sam Houston and Quanah Parker courtesy of Texas State Library and Archives Commission; Babe Zaharias courtesy of Babe Zaharias Foundation.

Printed in South Korea by Pacifica Communications
9 8 7 6 5 4 3

Library of Congress Cataloging-in-Publication Data

Parker, Laurie, 1963-
   Texas alphabet / written and illustrated by Laurie Parker.
   p. cm.
   ISBN 1-893062-17-1 (alk. paper)
     1. Texas—Juvenile literature. 2. English language—Alphabet—Juvenile literature. [1. Texas—Miscellanea. 2. Alphabet.] I. Title

   F386.3 .P37 2000
   976.4[E]—dc21   00-035291

QUAIL RIDGE PRESS
P. O. Box 123, Brandon, MS 39043
1-800-343-1583 • www.quailridge.com

Remember The ALAMO!

That's what we'll say
To get our state alphabet book underway...

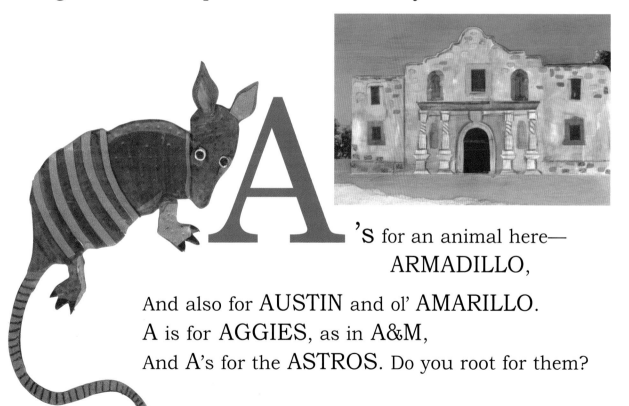

A's for an animal here—
ARMADILLO,

And also for AUSTIN and ol' AMARILLO.
A is for AGGIES, as in A&M,
And A's for the ASTROS. Do you root for them?

B is for BEEF and the best BARBECUE,

And BIG BEND and BISON and BLUEBONNETS, too.

B is for BUDDY. Oh Boy! BUDDY HOLLY,
And BIG TEX and BEAUMONT
                and BROWNSVILLE, by golly!

B's for Jim BOWIE, whom we still salute,
The BORDER

        the BRAZOS

                and BAYLOR to
                        BOOT!

BAYTOWN   BRYAN   BUFFALO   BROWNWOOD   BRADY

BAIRD   BASTROP   BORGER   BAY CITY   BRENHAM

BELLAIRE   BRECKENRIDGE   BOERNE   BURKBURNETT

Bb

BLOSSOM   BEEVILLE   BIG SPRING   BEDFORD   BELTON

CANYON   CUT AND SHOOT   COLLEGE STATION   CLUTE

CHANNELVIEW   CUERO   CEDAR HILL   CONROE

CLEBURNE   CROCKETT   COMFORT   COMANCHE

Cc

COPPERAS COVE   CARROLLTON   CORSICANA   COPPELL

C

is for COWBOYS—on gridiron and saddle,

COTTON BOWL, CACTUS, COYOTES, and CATTLE.
A tribe called the CADDO gave our state its name,
And there are more C words we Texans can claim...
Like CADILLAC RANCH, CORPUS CHRISTI, CORRAL,
The old CHISHOLM TRAIL and CAMINO REAL.
We've CAVERNS and CANYONS and lovely CLEAR LAKE,
The CHISOS

and CHILI

and CHICKEN-FRIED STEAK!

Dd

DENISON   DEER PARK   DE SOTO   DUNCANVILLE   DRAW

DUBLIN

DONNA

DAYTON

DEVINE

DUMAS

DICKINSON

DECATUR

DALHART

DILLEY

DENTON   DEL RIO   DIMMITT   DAISETTA   DIME BOX

D is for DALLAS—indeed, our "Big D,"
And the DOME of our Capitol—something to see.
D is for DOGWOODS and D is for DRAWL,
DEL RIO and DESERTS, but that isn't all.
It's for DAVY CROCKETT, whom Texans hold dear,
And don't forget DUDE RANCH—
that's what D's for here!

E's for EL PASO, ENCHANTED ROCK Park,
And Dwight EISENHOWER,
whose birthplace we mark.
EAGLE PASS...EDINBURG...EARTH...EULESS...ETTER...
They're all Texas places that start with this letter.

F is for FRIENDSHIP, and friendly we are,

And F's for our FOLKLORE well-known near and far.

F's for FORT BLISS, FORT SAM HOUSTON, FORT HOOD,
And for more than a few Texas things that are good...

FIESTAS and FESTIVALS,
FAMILIES and FUN,
FAJITAS and FOOTBALL,
but we are not done.

For F's for our FLAG,
our fantastic State FAIR,

And finally, for FORT WORTH—the West begins there!

FREDERICKSBURG   FALFURRIAS   FARMERS BRANCH   FLAT

FREER

FLOYDADA

FORT DAVIS

FLORESVILLE

Ff

FAIRFIELD

FREEPORT

FORNEY

FRITCH

FRIENDSWOOD   FLOWER MOUND   FORT STOCKTON   FRISCO

G

G's for some grand things of which Texans speak.

It's for GUADALUPE, our loftiest peak.

G is for GRAPEFRUITS we grow that are great,

And GERMAN influences
found in our state.

G's for the GULF—
that's where GALVESTON sits,
And GOLIAD,
          GOAT RANCHES,
GHOST TOWNS,
          and GRITS!

H

is for HOUSTON—a humongous place,
And for a rich HERITAGE we can embrace.
H is for "HOWDIES"
we say from the heart,

William H. HUDDLE's
historical art,

HILL COUNTRY,

HORSES,

the huge HUECO TANKS,
And all of our HEROES to whom we owe thanks.

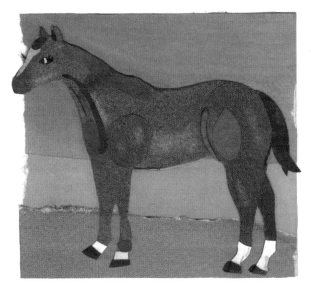

I

is for INTERSTATES...stretching for miles,

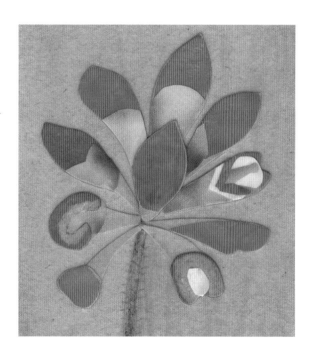

and
INDIAN
PAINTBRUSH

and

IRVING

and

ISLES.

KELLER
KINGWOOD
KAUFMAN
KINGSVILLE

JACINTO CITY
JEFFERSON
JACKSONVILLE

J's for the JOHNSON
SPACE CENTER. It's big!
And it's for JAVELINA, a kind of wild pig.
We have San JACINTO, and that has a J,
And so does JUNETEENTH—
that's a real joyous day!

K is for KING RANCH, best known for its size,
And KATHERINE Anne Porter, a writer we prize.

LIBERTY   LUFKIN   LIVE OAK   LAMPASAS   LEVELLAND

LOOP

LA GRANGE

LEWISVILLE

LA MARQUE

LA PORTE   LAKE JACKSON   LANCASTER   LLANO

L1

LOCKHART   LULING   LEAGUE CITY   LAMESA   LOVING

L is for LONE STAR.   What else starts with L?

LUBBOCK, LAREDO, and LONGVIEW as well.
   There's LADY BIRD Johnson, the late LBJ,
LEGENDS,
        LIVE MUSIC, and LONGHORNS. Hooray!
L's also for LUCKENBACH—quaint little place,
And LIVESTOCK

             and LASSOS

                    and LACKLAND Air Base.

M

is for MISSIONS—some centuries old,

And the strange MARFA LIGHTS—they're a sight to behold!

MIDLAND's an M town of which you have heard,

And M is for MOCKINGBIRD.
That's our state bird.

M is for MEXICO—
right smack next door,

MESQUITE
and MUSEUMS
and MAVERICKS
and more...

NASH

NAVASOTA

NORTH RICHLAND HILLS

NASSAU BAY

NADA

NEW BOSTON

N's for our own
NOLAN Ryan—nice guy!
And N's for the sculptress,
Elisabet NEY.
N is for NIMITZ, an admiral of fame,
And it's for NACOGDOCHES...
Now, that's a neat name!

O's for the OIL
that has helped our state grow,
And ODESSA and ORANGE—
two towns you might know.

P is for PANHANDLE—open and wide.

P's for PETROLEUM. P's for State PRIDE.
There are more things that make Texas special—all sorts...
PRAIRIES and PLAINS,

PADRE ISLAND,

and PORTS,
PINEY WOODS, PECOS, PECAN—our state tree,

And yep, PALO DURO! Those all start with P!

Q's for a favorite hereabouts—QUARTER HORSE.

And Q is for
Chief
QUANAH Parker,
of course.

R is for RANCHES
            spread over the land,
And R's for the long and renowned RIO GRANDE.
There's ROPIN' and RIDIN'—fun RODEO tricks,

    ROADRUNNERS,

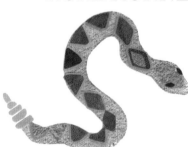

            RATTLESNAKES,

                    ROUTE 66...

And R is for RIVER WALK—just right for dining,
REPUBLIC and RANGERS and RIGS and REFINING.

ROUND ROCK   ROCKWALL   ROSENBERG   RAINBOW
RUSK
ROBSTOWN
RIO GRANDE CITY
RAYMONDVILLE
ROUND TOP
ROCKDALE
RICHMOND
RICHARDSON   ROWLETT   REFUGIO   RIO HONDO

ROUTE 66

Rr

SEGUIN   SULPHUR SPRINGS   SUGAR LAND   SAN MARCOS

SILVER   SEMINOLE   SAN BENITO   STEPHENVILLE

SHERMAN   SAN AUGUSTINE   SNYDER   SINTON

Ss

SAN ANGELO   SUNDOWN   SPRING   SWEETWATER   SILSBEE

 stands for SADDLE and STIRRUPS and STEER,

And SAM!

That is Houston and Rayburn 'round here.

S is for SPINDLETOP,
              SPURS,
                  "SAN ANTONE,"

And also for SIX FLAGS
              that our state has flown.

We still sing the praises of STARS here so bright,
              And our city SKYLINES are splendid at night!

T is the letter that stands for our state

And for many more things to which TEXANS relate...

Like TEJANO music and TEX MEX and TRUCKS,
And TYLER, whose roses are downright deluxe.

T is for TUMBLEWEED,

TEN-GALLON HAT,

and TEXAS TWO-STEP.

Have you ever done that?

TAHOKA   TEXARKANA   TERLINGUA   TURKEY   TERRELL

TAFT   THE COLONY   TEAGUE   TRINITY   TYE

THROCKMORTON   TELEPHONE   THREE RIVERS

Tt

TEXAS CITY   TOMBALL   TAYLOR   TEMPLE   TULIA

U

has the shape of a horseshoe; it's clear,
And it stands for
our fine
UNIVERSITIES here!

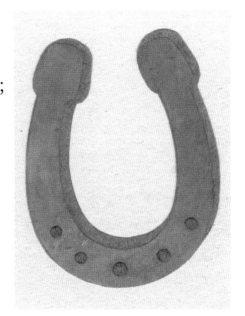

V

's for The **VALLEY**,
and vast **VINEYARDS**, too,
And V's for **VAQUERO**. That's like "Buckaroo!"

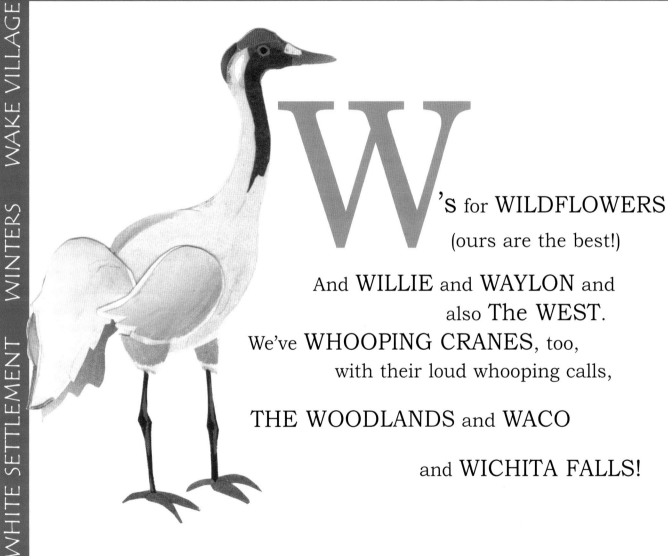

W's for WILDFLOWERS
(ours are the best!)
And WILLIE and WAYLON and
also The WEST.
We've WHOOPING CRANES, too,
with their loud whooping calls,

THE WOODLANDS and WACO

and WICHITA FALLS!

In TEXAS, there's one thing for which  can be—

Exactly! The ranch that we call

And now comes the next-to-last letter...YAHOO!

Of Y words in Texas, we'll mention just two:
The YSLETA Mission, and yes—YELLOW ROSE.
There's a song about that. Do Y'ALL know how it goes?

Yy

YORKTOWN   YOAKUM   YANCEY   YANTIS

Z's the last letter of all, so we gotta

salute

Babe ZAHARIAS,

ZOOS,

And ZAPATA!

That's A to Z, and that means we're done.
Wasn't our Texas state alphabet fun?!